To: ______________________________

From: ______________________________

Mfd. for © DaySpring Cards, Inc., Siloam Springs, AR 72761.

Made in China

# January 1

*By the grace of God, I am what I am.*

1 CORINTHIANS 15:10

# December 31

This isn't the end.
With the God who makes you
amazing, it's always only

*the beginning.*

# January 2

Has anyone told you lately
how amazing you are?
It's about time you heard it again.
I hear you saying, "Who me?"
I'm saying right back, "Yep, you."

# December 30

*I know* that you have what it takes to accomplish God's purpose for your life.

*I know* the people whose paths you cross are going to be blessed because of you.

*I know* that your life is a story being written by an Author who has more in store for you than either of us can even imagine.

# January 3

*You're already amazing...*
the one doing your thing,
making your difference,
being a glorious mess
that God can use.

# December 29

You're already amazing
because you belong to God,
because he has a plan for your life,
because with him there's
nothing you can't do.

# January 4

*You're already amazing...*
getting back up
when you fall down,
trying again
when it doesn't work out,
doing the hard, the different,
taking those steps of faith.

# December 28

You're already amazing because God made you, formed you, and lives within you.

# January 5

*You're already amazing...*
wonderfully made just like you are,
and on your way to becoming
all God made you to be.

# December 27

God never promised it would be easy
but He did promise you'll never be alone.
He has a plan for your life, your heart

*and it's good.*

# January 6

*You're already amazing...*
I see you squinting a little
at the page and thinking,
"That's for other women
but I'm not so sure about me."
Believe it, receive it, it's true.
This is for *you*.

# December 26

*Hello, you...*

wondering what's next,
where you're headed,
what might happen now.
There's One who knows the way.
Every step.
Every day.
Every moment.

# January 7

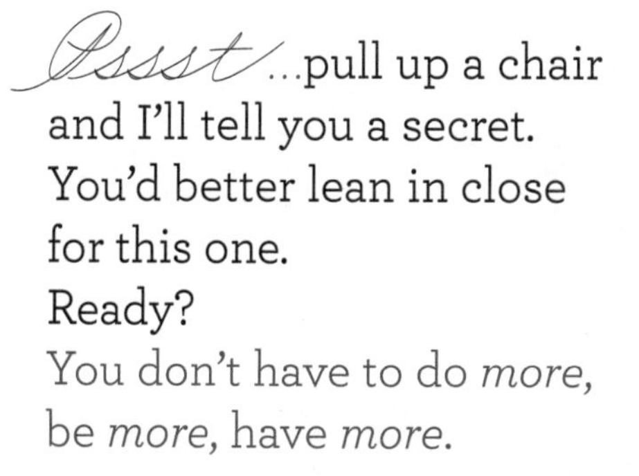

Pssst...pull up a chair
and I'll tell you a secret.
You'd better lean in close
for this one.
Ready?
You don't have to do *more*,
be *more*, have *more*.

# December 25

One day we'll stand before Jesus in heaven and we'll look back over our lives with a different perspective. The moments you lived in your strengths, the challenges you pushed through, the ways you made a difference—they'll all be something beautiful that you can give the One who gave everything for you.

# January 8

You're a daughter of God, a holy princess, a woman created with strengths you're yet to fully grasp and a story that's still being written by the divine Author himself.

# December 24

God promises us that in the end it will all be worth it and we'll understand everything we went through along the way. Jeremiah 29:11 says God has good plans for us, a hope and a future. Does that mean it will always be easy or what we want? Nope, not at all. What it does mean is that we can trust him—no matter what.

# January 9

If you really take hold of who you are and what you're called to do, there will be no stopping you. That's because there's no stopping Him *in you*—and He's got bigger plans for your life than you've even imagined.

# December 23

Your heart has a home—
and it's not a place
but a Person who
will never let you go.

# January 10

"Dear daughter," God whispers
to our hearts, "Come to me.
You are weary and burdened.
I will give you rest. You're already
pleasing to me."

# December 22

All that you fear holds you back
has been wiped away, forgiven,
covered up by grace.
And the One who created you,
knows you, calls you his own,
looks at you with love
and says, “You’re mine forever.”

# January 11

Yes, you matter.
No one can take your place.
God made just one *you*
and this world needs you
just as you are.

*You're loved.*

More than you know.
More than you see.
Deeper than you've even dared to dream.

# January 12

*I praise You because I am fearfully*
*and wonderfully made;*
*Your works are wonderful,*
*I know that full well.*

PSALM 139:14

# December 20

We spend a lot of time trying to figure out how God can love us and what that means. But all we really need to know is that He does.
Really.
Truly.
Just as you are.
As high as the sky.
More than you can even imagine.

# January 13

You're not only amazing.
You're enough.
You're beautiful.
You're wanted.
You're chosen.
You're called.
You've got what it takes...
not just to survive but to change the world.

# December 19

Embracing God's love isn't done with our heads but with our hearts. It's not about understanding but instead simply receiving.

# January 14

You ask, "Who told you
I'm already amazing?"
And I respond, "The only One
who really knows—
Someone Who Loves You."

# December 18

*I pray that you, being rooted and established in love, may have power, together with all the saints, to grasp how wide and long and high and deep is the love of Christ, and to know this love that surpasses knowledge—that you may be filled to the measure of all the fullness of God.*

EPHESIANS 3:17-19

# January 15

Our culture is obsessed with the 'it girl.' She's defined as a woman who has it all together—whatever "it" is at the moment. But when we look at the Kingdom it's a different story. There aren't 'it girls' (or guys). There are only 'is girls.' God looks at you and says, "*She is* loved, accepted, and valued. She is created just the way I wanted her to be."

# December 17

When we mess up it can feel as if the sky is going to crash down around us. But as much as it may seem like it, our lives aren't about us. They're about our Maker. And his love never changes.

# January 16

The Apostle Paul told early Christians that we're part of the body of Christ. Someone is a hand. Another person is a foot. There's no competition—only complementing and completion.

# December 16

As high as the heavens
are above the earth.
How high is that?
*Endless.*
That's the way
God's love for us is too.

# January 17

Part of the beauty of the body of Christ
is how different we are from each other.

# December 15

*For as high as the heavens are above the earth, so great is His love for those who fear Him.*

PSALM 103:11

# January 18

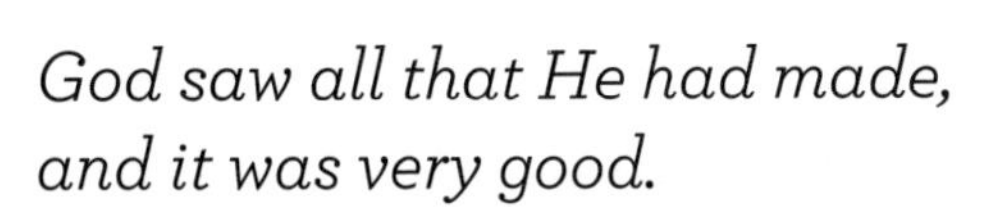

*God saw all that He had made,*
*and it was very good.*

GENESIS 1:31

# December 14

Move forward in faith,
into all you are and all he has for you.
You're already on your way.

# January 19

"God creates each of us to be uniquely who we are—just like each part of the body is unique too. We don't need more than one of a certain body part. Nor would we want more than one. Sure, we have two hands and two feet. But not even two *right* hands or two *left* feet. Each part of the body has a purpose that only it can fulfill. The same is true for us. That's a truth that's easy to understand *and easy to forget*."

JENNIFER LEEP

# December 13

Are you ready to take that next step?
You can do this, sweet girl.
With him.
In his *power.*
That power created the world,
spoke the stars into place,
spread the sea from one shore to another.
That's the power that lives in YOU.

# January 20

We're in pretty good company if we feel like we're not like most people. After all...
*Most people don't*...build an ark.
*Most people don't*...lead people through the desert to the Promised Land.
*Most people don't*...die on a cross to save the world.
But aren't we glad one person did each of these things?

# December 12

You've begun to move forward, to make changes, to recognize the incredible woman you are and become more of who God created you to be. And the enemy would love nothing more than to convince you it's too much, you can't do it, there's not enough time...the list is endless. But it's not true, dear friend. You can change. You can grow. You already have—don't let anything stand in your way.

# January 21

If most people don't do what you're doing and you're passionately pursuing Jesus with your life, then it's probably not the plan of man. There's probably the heartbeat of God somewhere within it.

# December 11

*Even so.*

Those two little words don't deny the difficulties or paste on a smile that says, "Everything is fine." They acknowledge life is hard. They recognize the obstacles. But in the end, they shift our gaze from what we see to Who we know. And that changes everything...*especially us.*

# January 22

We need you, *just you,* to fulfill that purpose, complete that project, bring that gift to the world in a way no one else can. Most people don't...but *you* do.

# December 10

*Even so.*

Yes, the situation is difficult and the obstacles seem insurmountable.

Even so, God will deliver me.

Yes, I left my comfort zone about 100 miles ago and all I want to do is eat a vat of chocolate.

Even so, God can use me.

Yes, it feels like the valley is dark, the mountains are high, and the enemy strong.

Even so, God is able to get me to the Promised Land.

Even so.

# January 23

*But he was pierced for our transgressions,*
*he was crushed for our iniquities;*
*the punishment that brought us peace was*
*upon him, and by his wounds we are healed.*

ISAIAH 53:5

# December 9

Dare to give what you've been given, to place it in the hands of the One who made you and who can make what you have to offer more than enough too.

# January 24

It seemed God whispered to my soul, "You think you have to take what's broken and make it perfect in order to be used by me. But I think in a completely different way. I took what was perfect, my Son, and made him broken so that you could be whole. And because you belong to him, your brokenness can bring healing to others too."

# December 8

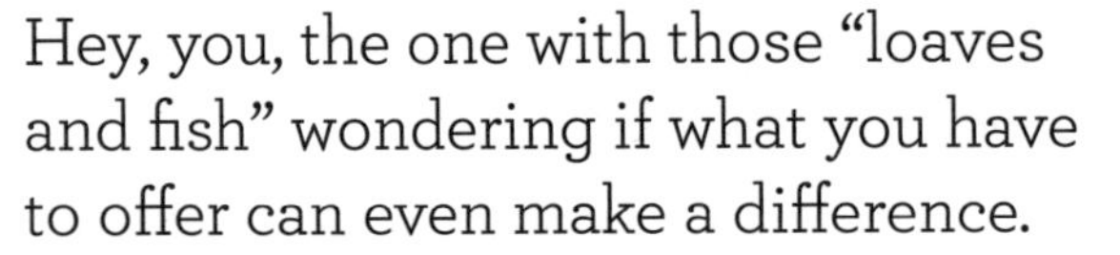

Hey, you, the one with those “loaves and fish” wondering if what you have to offer can even make a difference.

*Oh, yes, it can.*

We need you, just you, to open your hands and your heart.

# January 25

Angie Smith shared a story on her blog *Bring the Rain* about smashing a pitcher and then piecing it back together again after the loss of her daughter: "God, my ever-gracious God, was gentle and yet convicting as he explained. '*My dearest Angie. How do you think the world has seen me? If it wasn't for the cracks, I couldn't seep out the way I do. I chose the pitcher. I chose you, just as you are.*'"

# December 7

It's not about what we have to offer.
It's about Whose hands we place it in.
And those hands? We can place
our hearts safely there too.

# January 26

God knows how to put our hearts together again. It's not the same as before— but it's good. He fills those empty spaces with his grace and, surprisingly, joy.

# December 6

Not only is Jesus the supplier—
He is the multiplier too.

# January 27

"Who am I, *really*?"
Until we can answer that question,
it's hard to believe we're amazing.
I believe the desire to know who we
really are has been placed within
us by the Heart of Heaven itself.

## December 5

Jesus steps in, takes us by the hands,
looks into our hearts and says,
"*Daughter, you don't have to be enough
or have a lot. Only offer all you are,
all you have, to me. I will turn that into
abundance beyond all you can imagine.
All things are possible with me.*"

# January 28

God wants us to understand who he created us to be so that we can fulfill the purpose he has for our lives.

# December 4

With God, you have more than enough...
you have everything you need
and you're everything you need to be
for his purposes to prevail in your life.

# January 29

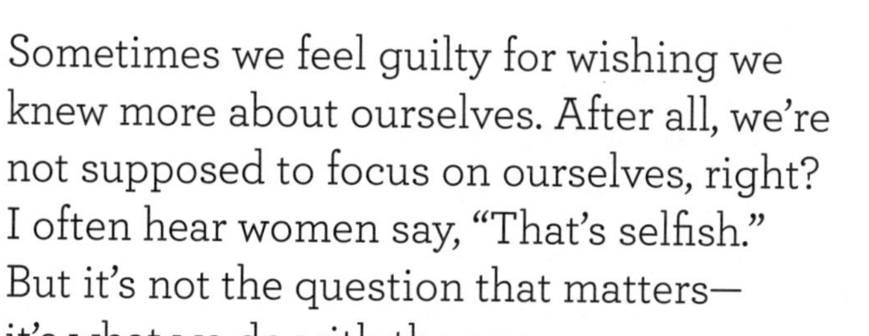

Sometimes we feel guilty for wishing we knew more about ourselves. After all, we're not supposed to focus on ourselves, right? I often hear women say, "That's selfish." But it's not the question that matters—it's what we do with the answer.

# December 3

*Good news:*

Nothing is impossible for you
because all things are possible
for the God who lives in you.
There's no obstacle too great,
no wall to high, no valley too low.
You can get through it, over it,
beyond it together.

# January 30

If you want to understand yourself just so that you can do whatever you'd like for your personal gain, then it's self-centered. If your intent is to love God, others, and yourself more, then knowing who you are is one of the most unselfish things you can do.

# December 2

What does faith sound like
in our everyday lives?
"This seems impossible for me.
But nothing is impossible
for the God who lives in me.
That means all things really
are possible for me too.
I can do this with Him."

# January 31

Discovering our strengths is like mining for diamonds. We know they're in there—we've just got to find them and bring them into the light.

# December 1

Let's believe that in us,
through us, in spite of us...
With God all things are
possible. Matthew 19:26

# February 1

You've got strengths.
I know it. God does too.
After all, he's the One
who placed them within you.

# November 30

There is nothing God can't do through
a heart fully surrendered to Him.
*Nothing.*
Lead an entire nation through a desert.
Knock down a giant with a single stone.
Fulfill His purpose for your life.

# February 2

*A strength is a personal characteristic that can be used on behalf of God in service to others.* Usually they're present throughout our lives but can be enhanced through experience or training. Strengths are part of *who we are* while skills are more about *what we do.*

# November 29

*Many are the plans in a man's heart,*
*but it's the Lord's purpose that prevails.*

PROVERBS 19:21

# February 3

How did you get your strengths?
God created you with them.
You are "fearfully and wonderfully made"
(Psalm 139:14).
Then he allows life experiences to
develop your strengths even more.

# November 28

I'm still quick to protest, "But I have so many weaknesses!" And then I remember that every promise given and every truth declared was for us, all of us, and none of us have it together. Our humanity isn't too much for God.

# February 4

Our brains are actually beautifully wired by God to approach life in certain ways.

"By the age of three each of your hundred billion neurons have formed fifteen thousand synaptic connections with other neurons....Your pattern of threads, extensive, intricate and unique, is woven."

MARCUS BUCKINGHAM AND DONALD O. CLIFTON,
*NOW DISCOVER YOUR STRENGTHS*

# November 27

I'm sure you remember the story of Peter walking on water with Jesus. Peter starts off well, takes a few steps, and begins to sink. Jesus asks, "Why did you doubt?"
I pause and ponder, "Who did Peter doubt? Jesus or himself?"
And it seems there's a whisper in response...
*Same thing.*
What I mean is this..."I no longer live but Christ lives in me" (Galatians 2:20).

# February 5

Our divinely created strengths are actually supported by our weaknesses because if we were good at everything we wouldn't focus on much of anything.

# November 26

You don't have to be afraid or hold back—
just hold out your heart to
the One who promises
to complete the good work he's
already started in you.

# February 6

Let's celebrate who we are...
fearfully and wonderfully made,
strengths and weaknesses
woven together just right.

# November 25

*All you are,*
everything God created you to be,
becomes a gift when placed in his hands.
There's nothing he can't mold, shape,
redeem, form into something beautiful.

# February 7

We tell ourselves, "I have to ALWAYS be friendly." Or "I should NEVER miss an opportunity to be kind." Then when we miss the mark, we're quick to condemn ourselves. But even in our areas of strength, we'll mess up. We'll fall short. We'll make mistakes. That's why there's grace.

# November 24

God really can use all of you—strengths, weaknesses, imperfections, and challenges. The only time that can't happen is when we refuse to give an area of our lives to him. But whatever we place in his hands, he can lovingly make into something useful and even beautiful.

# February 8

We don’t have to muster up the power to live in our strengths. Philippians 4:13 says, “I can do all things through Christ who strengthens me.”

# November 23

In the times when we can't seem to transform our weaknesses to strengths, God can still make up for (and even use!) our imperfections.

# February 9

Jesus is the source of our strengths and he's also the one who enables us to live in them each day.

# November 22

That's the thing about light—
we can't save it up
or carry it back.
It's always for now,
always for where we are today,
because it flows
from the One who is *I am.*
We can only reflect him
in the here and now
because that's where He is.

# February 10

We don't have to force ourselves to always be "on" all the time. Instead our focus can be on remaining "in" Christ.

# November 21

I'm thinking of you today...
the past pulling at your sleeves,
the future tugging at your hands.
Take a deep breath.
Just for a moment.
Just in *this* moment.
Ah, yes, look at you—
beautiful you.
The sunlight of *now*
is on your face,
the glow within you is spilling out too.

# February 11

Ask God to use your strengths to glorify him and serve others. And if you mess up, ask forgiveness and keep on going.

# November 20

The temptation will always be to say, "After I..." or "When this happens then I'll..." but life doesn't work that way. You, your circumstances, your life will never be everything you want them to be. Don't let that stop you. Embrace this moment. Be who you are. You're the best gift you can give the world.

# February 12

*Be gentle with yourself.*

When we're tired, hungry, lonely, or afraid then our strengths can quickly flip to the other extreme. Passion becomes irritability. Sensitivity turns into worry.

# November 19

What you have to give, what you have to share with the world, is far too important to be missed. We need you to be you—not tomorrow, next week, next year—but where you are at this very second.

## February 13

If you find yourself having a reaction that's not helpful, just stop and take a deep breath. Rather than wishing you were different, stop and say, "I'm getting away from my strengths right now. Jesus, help me."

# November 18

We may think back with regret on who we wish we'd been. We may look forward with fear about who we might (or might not become). But the only place where we can offer ourselves, where God can use us, is the moment we're in right now.

# February 14

Ask yourself, "What do I need to change this reaction and respond out of one of my strengths instead?" Ask God for help and then take action.

# November 17

This present moment is the only place we can fully experience God because he is *I am*. We find him not in the future or in the past. Instead we find him right here with us, beside us, in us. When we take hold of that, take hold of him, then we become all we're called to be today.

## February 15

*When you attack yourself you side with the enemy*. God is always for you—that means you can be too.

# November 16

We only get one you. There has never been, and will never be, another you in this world. God doesn't have a back-up plan or replacement policy. We don't need a copy of someone else—we need the one-and-only original you.

# February 16

We'll all slip out of our strengths at times. The key is just getting back into them as quickly as possible. Receiving God's grace and giving it to ourselves speeds up that process.

# November 15

Out of all of history, God chose this time for you to be on earth. He knew the exact second you would enter this world with a cry and change it forever. In between the laundry, the endless trips to the office, the mundane parts of being human we can forget that we're part of a bigger story, a greater plan.

# February 17

The goal is not perfection. It's simply to be in an intimate relationship with Christ each day, fully embrace who he created us to be, and seek to fulfill the purpose he has for us.

*Beautiful you,*

deeply loved, chosen, called,
and on your way Home
to the One who cherishes you
*so much more* than your
heart can even know.

# February 18

God is our greatest strength—and the One who enables us to live out all the other strengths he's placed within us.

# November 13

You're made for *more*...
more of Jesus,
more of his presence in your life,
more of all he has to offer.
Joy, hope, peace, grace, goodness.
And right there in the middle of it all is you.

# February 19

*Hey, you...*

The one wondering if you've
got strengths.
*You do.*
The one questioning if God
really even wants to use you.
*He does.*

# November 12

God will give us the courage to be who He made us and to cross the finish line into eternity with a smile on our faces knowing we ran well every step of the way.

# February 20

You've got gifts to offer the world.
Things that are good and right and true.
No one else can make a
difference like you can.
*Like you already are.*

# November 11

What we've been talking about
isn't making our lives perfect.
Instead it's about learning to turn to
Jesus when our hearts feel a longing
for things to be different in our lives.

# February 21

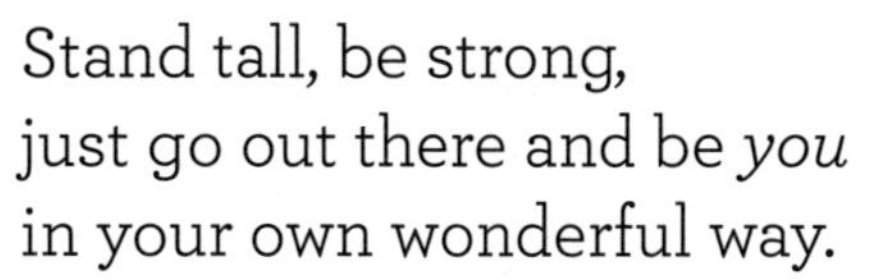

Stand tall, be strong,
just go out there and be *you*
in your own wonderful way.

*Today.*

# November 10

*He has made everything beautiful in its time. He has also set eternity in the hearts of men; yet they cannot fathom what God has done from beginning to end.*

ECCLESIASTES 3:11

# February 22

Strengths are made to be expressed. We call those expressions *skills. A skill is a strength expressed in a specific way that builds up others and benefits the Kingdom.*

# November 9

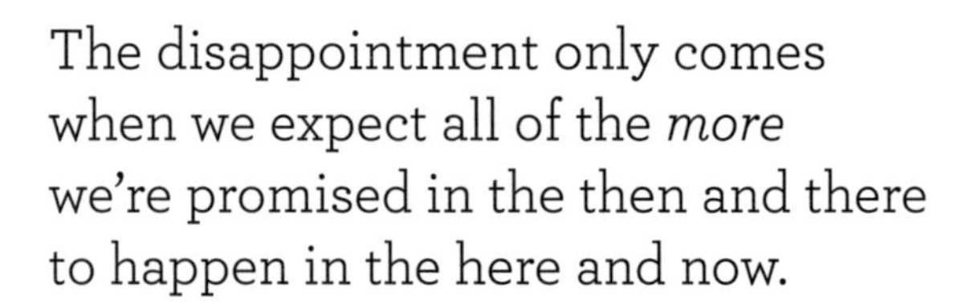

The disappointment only comes
when we expect all of the *more*
we're promised in the then and there
to happen in the here and now.

# February 23

"I have filled him with the Spirit of God, with skill, ability and knowledge in all kinds of crafts" (Exodus 31:3). This verse reveals that God's hand is in our skills, in the ordinary things we do. And they matter. *A lot.*

# November 8

You *are* made for more than this.
The trouble isn't feeling that way—
it's expecting it all to happen here.
That discontent within you is a
homing beacon, reminding of Eden
and redirecting you toward heaven.

# February 24

*You are a chosen people, a royal priesthood, a holy nation, a people belonging to God, that you may declare the praises of him who called you out of darkness into his wonderful light.*

1 PETER 2:9

# November 7

You are valuable.
And you have so much
of value to offer.
*Take care of you.*
And finish well.

# February 25

While strengths stay consistent throughout our lives, the skills that display them vary depending on the season we're in and the specific assignment God has given us.

# November 6

"Well done, good and faithful servant!" (Matthew 25:23). That's what it's all about in the end. Receiving and then investing so that one day we too can hear from the lips of the one our hearts love,

*"Well done."*

# February 26

While what we do may change,
the reason we do it stays the same.
"Whatever you do, do it all for the
glory of God" (1 Corinthians 10:31).

# November 5

*Love the Lord your God with all your heart and with all your soul and with all your mind and with all your strength....*
*Love your neighbor as yourself.*
*There is no commandment greater than these.*

MARK 12:30-31

# February 27

King David had the skill of shepherding. He did that first with sheep and then as a ruler of God's people. Peter had the skill of fishing—first with actual fish and then with hearts. God will use you in a lot of different ways throughout your life.

# November 4

If you haven't figured it out yet:
*you're amazing because you're God's creation and he lives in you.* You're valuable because you belong to him. You're worth investing in because he paid the ultimate price for you. Dare to take the risk. Love yourself because he loves you.

# February 28

Here's a little confession: I can tend to focus too much on my skills, especially in the busy times of my life. I spin my wheels, wear myself out, and try to do everything at once. When I finally slow down enough to hear God's voice, it seems what he often whispers to my heart is, *"I want your heart more than your hands."*

# November 3

It's okay to take care of yourself because you are someone's beloved. You are the bride of Christ. You belong to the One who hung the stars in place, who knows every detail of your day, who is waiting for the moment when you're finally together forever. You matter to him. He wants the best for you.

# February 29

Yes, our skills matter. Yes, they are important to God's purpose for our lives. But in the end what he wants most is simply *us*. Our hearts. Our dreams. Our days. Then what we do with our skills is just a natural response—and ordinary activities such as cooking or cleaning become just as sacred as leading a church or going on a mission trip.

# November 2

The end goal of taking care of ourselves isn't simply to be happy or personally satisfied. It's so that we can love God, others, and ourselves.

# March 1

It seems God has been whispering
that I need to look at the
ordinary with new eyes.
That all that *small* is really BIG.
And what we do every day
matters more than we know,
more than we see.

# November 1

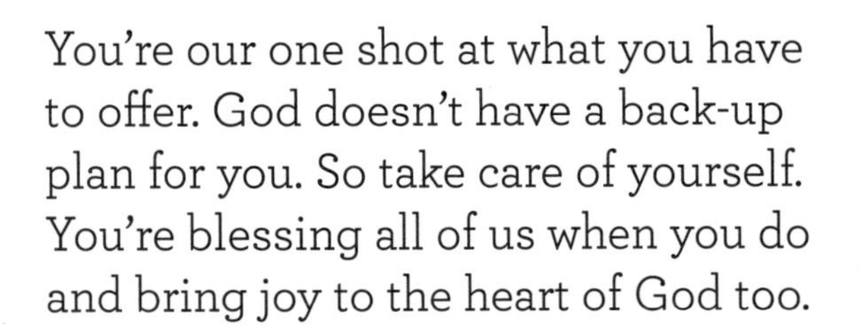

You're our one shot at what you have to offer. God doesn't have a back-up plan for you. So take care of yourself. You're blessing all of us when you do and bring joy to the heart of God too.

# March 2

*You are making a difference.*
You deserve to be applauded—
for just digging in, doing what you do,
keeping at it no matter what.

# October 31

You are worth investing in, sweet sister.
You are a daughter of the King,
a holy princess, a woman with a
purpose in this world and a calling
on your life. You are of infinite value
and no one can take your place.

# March 3

From the bottom of my heart...
*thank you*
for all you do.
(I've got a feeling God
is grateful for it too.)

# October 30

Telling women they're not allowed to receive is one of the subtlest and most dangerous tactics of the enemy. He might not be able to make us ineffective by falling into a major sin but he can accomplish the same thing by driving us to become utterly empty and exhausted.

# March 4

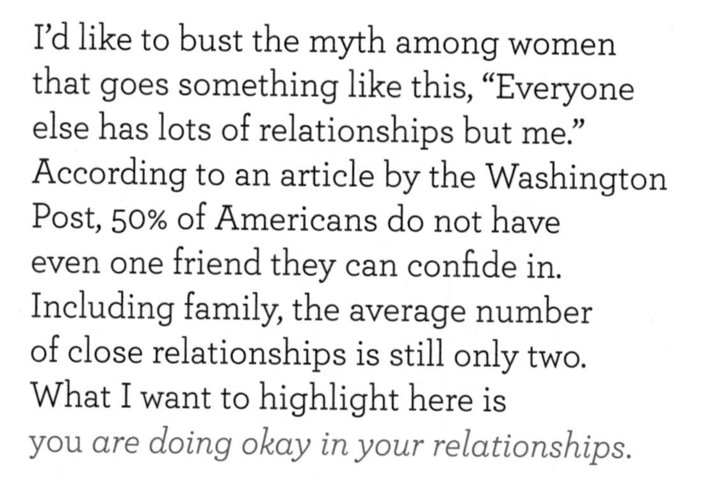

I'd like to bust the myth among women that goes something like this, "Everyone else has lots of relationships but me." According to an article by the Washington Post, 50% of Americans do not have even one friend they can confide in. Including family, the average number of close relationships is still only two. What I want to highlight here is *you are doing okay in your relationships.*

# October 29

It grieves God when we treat ourselves poorly just like it would if we treated one of our sisters in Christ that way. If someone were harsh or demanding with a close friend of yours, you would come to her defense. If she were exhausted or burned-out, you would try to help her get some rest. Sometimes we need to do the same for ourselves.

# March 5

When we look at the life of Jesus, we see he had different types of relationships. He had three disciples who were closest to Him, then the twelve, the forty, and the multitudes. Our relationships will vary with the seasons and stages of our lives.

# October 28

When God looks at his daughters,
he sees each of us the same.
He wants us to love ourselves the
way we love others in our lives.

# March 6

Connections to others impact our lives now and our legacies forever. As DaySpring cofounder Dean Kerns once said, "All we take with us into eternity are our relationships with God and each other."

# October 27

If we wait until we're perfect to receive, then it's never going to happen. You can receive now because you are God's child, dearly loved, redeemed, chosen and cherished. You can receive not because of what you do but because of who you are in him.

# March 7

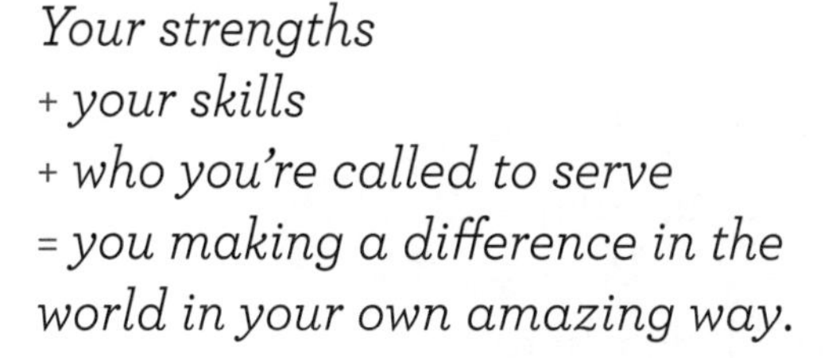

*Your strengths*
*+ your skills*
*+ who you're called to serve*
*= you making a difference in the world in your own amazing way.*

# October 26

Sometimes we push others away or withhold what we need from ourselves because we don't believe we've earned it. When we're better, skinnier, wealthier, holier, or a better mom, wife, friend then we'll deserve to receive. We treat receiving as a reward. But God clearly tells us that receiving is always about grace.

# March 8

"Lord," I asked, "Why do women
feel as if we're not enough?"
It seemed I heard a whisper in
response, "Because they're not...
in me you are so much more."
We are much more than pretty...
we are wonderfully made.
We are much more than likeable...
we are deeply loved.
We are much more than okay...
we are daughters of the King.

# October 25

You bless others by letting them give to you—just like you feel blessed when you give to them.

# March 9

I think the enemy tricks us into believing we are not enough because he knows if we discover the truth we'll be unstoppable.

Jesus doesn't want us to be exhausted. He doesn't expect us to be all things to all people. So take a deep breath, lean back into his love, and ask him what your heart needs to be filled with today.

# March 10

We are chosen, cherished, created women who have all we need to fulfill God's plans for our lives.

# October 23

*Come to me, all you who are weary and burdened, and I will give you rest.*

MATTHEW 11:28

# March 11

God has made us just as he wants us to be. We have something to offer that no one else can bring...and the world is waiting.

# October 22

Go out there and run the race he's got for you, girl. The world is watching and heaven is cheering you on (*and I am too*).

# March 12

Girls, let's stop shaking in our boots and
instead start standing tall for him together.
Let's use our strengths, skills, and
relationships to make a difference.
Let's be who we are, *really*.
I can't do it alone—are you with me?

# October 21

*I run in the path of Your commands,*
*for you have set my heart free.*

PSALM 119:32

# March 13

*His divine power has given us everything we need for life and godliness through our knowledge of him.*

2 PETER 1:3

# October 20

The best place to start is with one small step. It's the only way to bigger things with God. As Jesus said, "Whoever can be trusted with very little can also be trusted with much" (Luke 16:10).

# March 14

The scene is set. God has created the world in seven glorious days. Adam and Eve live in Paradise. And then the devil shows up with a single question: "Did God really say...?" Insecurity makes its debut. Eve responds, then reconsiders. "The woman was convinced" (Genesis 3:6). Everything changes forever.

# October 19

Good news:
**Yes, Jesus says we can**
**do all things through him—**
but he never says
we have to do it all!

# March 15

"Did God really say you have what it takes?"
"Did God really say you're loved?"
"Did God really say who you are is okay?"
Like Eve, I often respond, reconsider,
become convinced. What if Eve had
said, "Yep, God sure did say that
and I'm not listening to another
word. Hit the road, buster."?
What if *we* said that?

# October 18

We can all do a lot if we just do a little.

And with God, there's *nothing* that's impossible for us.

# March 16

"*Yes*, God really did say I can do all things through Christ." (Philippians 4:13)

"*Yes*, God really did say he loves me with an everlasting love." (Jeremiah 31:3)

"*Yes*, God really did say I am fearfully and wonderfully made." (Psalm 139:14)

# October 17

Sometimes we're so busy pushing forward that we forget to stop and thank God for how far he's taken us. God is there for us in hard times and he loves rejoicing with us too. So let him share the joy.

# March 17

I used to think there had to be a silver bullet that would kill my insecurity and replace it with confidence. I now believe that because we're all Eve's daughters this is something we'll face throughout our lives. Can we have victory? Yes, my sisters, we can. But it's not a one-time, easy fix. It's a battle.

# October 16

God gave us grace for a reason—he knew we'd need it. And he promises an endless supply. What matters most to him isn't that you always get it right but instead that you stay right by his side.

# March 18

Let's drop that guilt that we struggle with insecurity, okay? Even Jesus was tempted and he was perfect. We're all going to wrestle with our identities, feel drawn to insecurity, and want to fill those holes within us in other ways. That's not a sin. What matters is what we do next.

# October 15

*Seek first his kingdom and his righteousness and all of these things will be added to you as well.*

MATTHEW 6:33

# March 19

We have a choice between living in
the truth or giving in to the flesh.
And what we pick ultimately shapes
the course of our lives and our selves.

# October 14

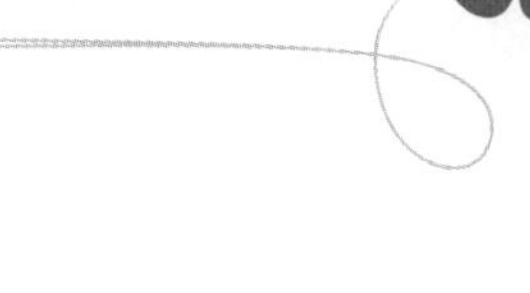

Change is outward while growth is inward. By figuring out how your goal fits with something deep inside you, you will be much more motivated to do what you can to accomplish it.

# March 20

From the moment we take our first breath as a beautiful baby girl the enemy wants to suffocate our souls with the question, "Did God really say...?" As our lives unfold, all of us experience the lies that come from that question in many different ways.

# October 13

God does ask us to do really hard things sometimes. And if that's the case, then we need to obey. But it seems we often use our energy and emotion on things that don't matter as much. Then when he does give us a big assignment, we're already exhausted. We need to be intentional about using what we've got in the most effective way so we can be ready for whatever is ahead in God's plans for us!

# March 21

We all have lies we carry around inside us. Usually they're so familiar we don't even pay much attention to them. Pause for a moment and ask God to show you some of the lies you've believed about yourself.

# October 12

Jesus said if we have faith as a mustard seed then we can move mountains. Have you seen a mustard seed? I was shocked the first time I did! Those things are *tiny*. It seems the point isn't how much we have on our own but whose hands we place it in. God knows how to turn our little bit into a whole lot.

# March 22

Whoever said "sticks and stones may break my bones but words will never hurt me" must not have experienced childhood. Sentences slung at our souls wound deeply. God wants to heal those hurts.

# October 11

Someone once told me that coming to the point where change happens is like adding one drop of water to a bucket every day. One day the bucket just overflows, but it's all the little drops along the way that make it happen.

# March 23

A woman accused is brought to Jesus.
The leaders are ready to stone her.
But Jesus "stooped down and wrote
in the dust" with his finger....
Now we stand as women accused.
The enemy is ready to throw stones at us.
In the dust of our hearts, I picture Jesus
writing truth that covers those words...

*Loved Accepted Chosen*

*Mine*

# October 10

We often get caught up in thinking
we have to do something really big to
achieve our goals, but sometimes the
little things really can make a difference.

## March 24

Others may speak into our lives.
But Jesus has the final say.

# October 9

Every runner has a rhythm that works best for her. You're the same way. When we set out to make changes, we need to be sure we're moving to be more of who God made us—not more like someone else.

# March 25

Jesus covers the lies with love.
May he heal us and help us to believe.

# October 8

This isn't about self-improvement.
It's about aligning our lives with love
in the way God created us to do.
To do that, we need a lot of grace
and an approach that makes sense
based on who God made us.

# March 26

Whatever the source of the lie,
God's intent remains the same:
to replace those lies with truth.

# October 7

We are running "the race marked out *for us*." That means we're only concerned about the obstacles *in our lane*. If someone feels she needs to do something then let her do it—it's probably in her lane. But that doesn't mean it's in yours.

# March 27

*Who shall separate us from the love of Christ? Shall trouble or hardship or persecution or famine or nakedness or danger or sword? As it is written: "For your sake we face death all day long; we are considered as sheep to be slaughtered." No, in all these things we are more than conquerors through him who loved us.*

ROMANS 8:35-37

# October 6

Everything that hinders.
Sin that so easily tangles.
Those are the obstacles God wants
us to clear out of our paths.
You can stop worrying about
everything else.

Read that again, girl.
*You can stop worrying about*
*everything else.*

# March 28

*For I am convinced that neither death nor life, neither angels nor demons, neither the present nor the future, nor any powers, neither height nor depth, nor anything else in all creation, will be able to separate us from the love of God that is in Christ Jesus our Lord.*

ROMANS 8:38-39

## October 5

Dare to embrace who you are.
Dare to do those weird things you do.
Dare to trust God's whispers into your life more than the demands of the world around you about "the right way."
You have the Holy Spirit within you and he will show you what you need to change in a way that's gentle, life-giving, and affirming.

# March 29

"By one sacrifice he has made perfect forever those who are being made holy" (Hebrews 10:14). What? I've already been made perfect? I thought at first my Bible might have a typo. But it turns out it's true. I've already been made perfect. And so have you.

# October 4

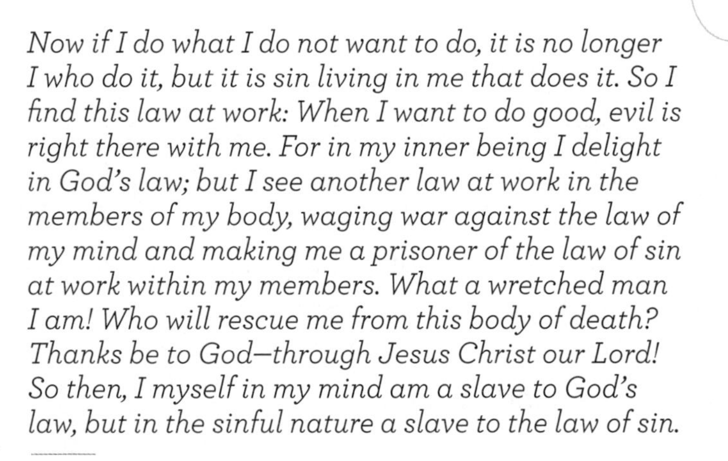

*Now if I do what I do not want to do, it is no longer I who do it, but it is sin living in me that does it. So I find this law at work: When I want to do good, evil is right there with me. For in my inner being I delight in God's law; but I see another law at work in the members of my body, waging war against the law of my mind and making me a prisoner of the law of sin at work within my members. What a wretched man I am! Who will rescue me from this body of death? Thanks be to God—through Jesus Christ our Lord! So then, I myself in my mind am a slave to God's law, but in the sinful nature a slave to the law of sin.*

ROMANS 7:20-25

# March 30

Here's how it works: There's only One who is perfect. To be perfect, I'd have to be him. But wait—"I no longer live, but Christ lives in me" (Galatians 2:20). When I gave my life to Jesus, he gave his to me too. In God's eyes, I'm as perfect as Christ.

# October 3

When we find ourselves entangled in sin, we can ask forgiveness, turn away from it, and get back on the path to keep going in our race. This battle with sin isn't a one-time fix. As Apostle Paul tells us, it's a step-by-step reliance on Christ.

# March 31

The Hebrew word for “perfect” is different than our typical western definition. It actually speaks more to the concept of being “complete” and we are all we need to be in Christ.

# October 2

You have a gift to offer the world, a calling only you can fulfill, a race only you can run. Throw off everything that hinders and move forward in all God has for you.

# April 1

Does being made perfect in Christ mean we're off the hook and can do whatever we want? Nope, that's where the second part of the verse from Hebrews comes in. We've been made perfect—check—but we're still in the process of being made holy. God's goal in our lives is *growth*.

# October 1

*Let us throw off everything that hinders and the sin that so easily entangles, and let us run with perseverance the race marked out for us. Let us fix our eyes on Jesus, the author and perfecter of our faith.*

HEBREWS 12:1-2

# April 2

So what's the difference between growth and our typical idea of "perfection"?

Perfectionism is all-or-nothing.
Growth is little-by-little.
Perfectionism is all about the goal.
Growth is more about the journey.
Perfectionism is about outward appearances.
Growth is about what happens on the inside.
Perfectionism is about what we do.
Growth is about who we're becoming.

# September 30

Are we to be responsible stewards of our lives, time, emotions, energy, and resources? Yes, of course. But how that looks in our daily lives is going to be as unique as we are. You have a purpose no one else does and how that unfolds will look different than any other woman in your life.

# April 3

*The path of the righteous is like the first gleam of dawn, shining ever brighter till the full light of day.*

PROVERBS 4:18

# September 29

What I mean is that we put a lot of pressure on ourselves to do things a certain way and/or to do it all. But God doesn't put those standards on us. Remember how we talked about expectations being like living under the law? Well, the woman-made standards in our lives are the same way.

# April 4

We go through peaks and valleys. We make some progress and then slip up. When that happens *it emotionally feels like we're all the way back at the bottom*. But we're not—we're farther along than we were before. We've gained new wisdom, developed our strengths a bit more, and leaned a little harder into God.

# September 28

The trees stretch out their arms. *And we stretch out our hearts.* I close my eyes and imagine the arms of One Who Loves Us reaching back, always finding us, always willing to carry us, always reminding us that life is about love—giving it, receiving it, gloriously growing until our hearts are Home.

# April 5

God covers our sins with the blood of his Son. Then he takes our hands, calls to our hearts, and says, "Let's go! I want to share life with you...just as you are, every step of the way."

# September 27

I'm looking at the trees in my backyard as I write these words.... I imagine for a moment that each leaf is a little bit of love. And I think of you—how you're out there growing too. Day after day, year after year, simply reaching a little higher toward heaven, drawing closer to God's heart.

# April 6

*Perfect love casts out fear. 1 John 4:18*
I don't have to be perfect.
I only need to be perfectly loved.
And I am.
*So are you.*

# September 26

What God wants most of all is you.
Just as you are. Then he'll show you
how he wants to use your life to partner
with him in fulfilling his purposes.
It won't be a burden but instead a glorious
adventure—with plenty of room for
mistakes, growth, and joy along the way.

# April 7

Women were created by God to be inherently relational. This means we're always checking in, asking ourselves, "How's she doing? How's she doing? How's SHE doing?" This is a reflection of our tender hearts and compassionate natures. It's a beautiful thing that makes us excellent mamas, wives, and friends. Where we get tripped up is when we follow that first question with, "How am I doing compared with her?"

# September 25

If you're loving God, others, and yourself
then *you're already doing enough.*

*That's right.*

And you're already amazing
because you are God's creation,
his child, and he lives in you.
Sounds scandalous, doesn't it?
But it's true.

# April 8

If we fall short compared to
others, then we're insecure.
If we're doing better, then we're prideful.
If someone else's life seems harder,
then we don't feel entitled to our pain.
God's answer? Focus on him
and his plan for your life.

# September 24

*You are free.*

Free to love.
Free to live in joy.
Free to be who you are.

# April 9

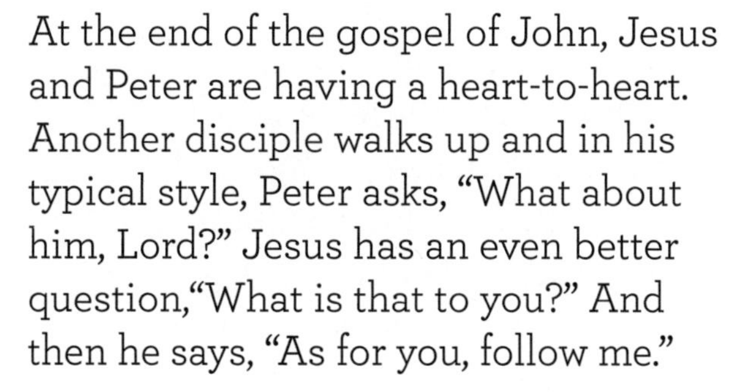

At the end of the gospel of John, Jesus and Peter are having a heart-to-heart. Another disciple walks up and in his typical style, Peter asks, “What about him, Lord?” Jesus has an even better question,“What is that to you?” And then he says, “As for you, follow me.”

# September 23

We might think that Jesus could have gotten a lot more accomplished if God had just let him get started sooner. But God isn't interested in how much we can do. If he can create the world in seven days with a few words then getting it done isn't an issue for him! Instead God is interested in our doing only what he's asked us to do, when he wants us to do it, and most of all to simply live in love along the way.

# April 10

Your story and strengths belong to you. God doesn't compare it (or you) to anyone else and you don't have to either. *Big sigh of relief.*

# September 22

We tend to think there's a pinnacle to our purpose, a high point we have to reach. But God cares more about the journey and our partnership with him in the process.

# April 11

Let's go for these three steps:
share, care, prayer.
And skip the compare.

# September 21

Whatever you are wired to do by God,
you'll find a way to do where you are—
and ALL of that is equally important to him.

# April 12

There might be some part of you that God has said is "fearfully and wonderfully made" (Psalm 139) but you're just not quite sure about that yet. Women seem to be pretty good at agreeing with God unless he's talking nice about us. Can I get an '*amen*'?

# September 20

As you let go of some things you're doing out of fear, it may seem as if a void opens up in your life. Our expectations are often also our *motivations*. The goal is to replace those expectations (the law) with the same thing Jesus did and what we've talked about all along—*love*.

# April 13

One of the biggest lies the enemy tries to tell us is that we don't have anything worthwhile to offer. Girls we do. And God says it's *good*.

# September 19

We can sift through our schedules and ask, “Does that really belong there? Is this a glimmer of false security? Is fear compelling me to do this?” We filter, sort, pay close attention. We toss away what is not of him and deeply treasure all that remains. Then we hold it up to the light and polish it until it shines even more brightly—and we do too.

# April 14

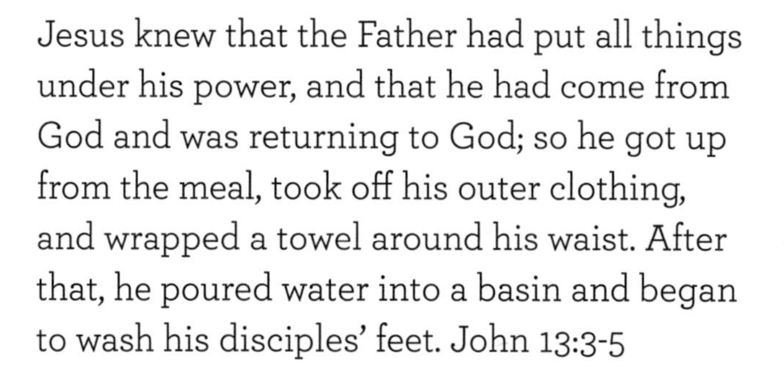

Jesus knew that the Father had put all things under his power, and that he had come from God and was returning to God; so he got up from the meal, took off his outer clothing, and wrapped a towel around his waist. After that, he poured water into a basin and began to wash his disciples' feet. John 13:3-5

Did you catch that first line? *Jesus was secure in who he was and whose he was and that enabled him to freely serve.*

# September 18

We look at our lives closely, like one mining for gold. We are of great worth, amazing women of God, and that means what we allow into our lives should be of value too.

# April 15

There's a myth that goes something like this, "Confidence will make you selfish." We fear becoming prideful, forgetting others, pursuing our own agendas. But here's the secret Jesus shows us: True confidence leads to service.

# September 17

Do we have to let go of all God's given? No, but we hold it loosely. We surrender. We say, "Not my will but yours be done."

# April 16

Insecurity does just what it sounds like, *turns us inward*. We focus on ourselves, our appearance, our house, our talents... you get the picture. I imagine you really want to do all you can to help, serve, be humble. Me too. If so, then we need to be secure, confident, assured that we're loved.

Easy? Not at all.

Life changing? Yes, ma'am.

# September 16

At one point in my life, it seemed God kept emptying my hands of so much. I asked, "Why are you doing that?" And I slowly came to realize God has to empty us of ourselves before he can fill us with him.

# April 17

Pride is really just another form of insecurity. It's an effort to puff ourselves up so we seem bigger (and therefore are safer). If we want to become more unselfish, then we've got to believe what God says about us. Because when we do, we'll be able to stop looking inward and instead focus upward and outward on him as well as others.

# September 15

Begin asking God to heal your heart so that you can do so more out of love and less from fear.

# April 18

As we lean into God's love and ask him to show us a new way of living then our fear will go away. I promise. And what's even better, God promises. "For God did not give us a spirit of timidity, but a spirit of power, of love and of self-discipline" (2 Timothy 1:7). That sounds a lot like true confidence to me.

# September 14

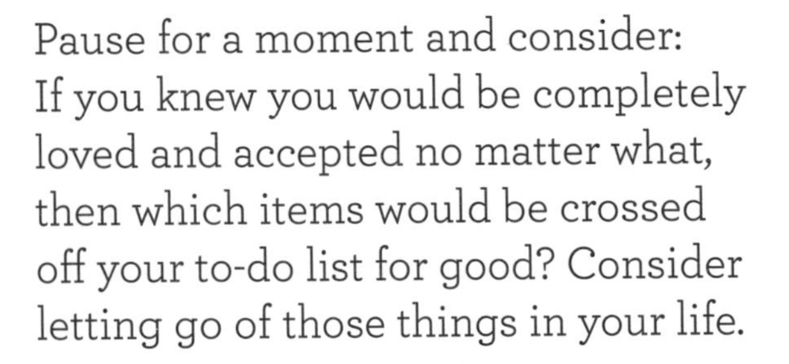

Pause for a moment and consider:
If you knew you would be completely
loved and accepted no matter what,
then which items would be crossed
off your to-do list for good? Consider
letting go of those things in your life.

# April 19

We tend to accept what others say
about us as the truth about who we are.
And it may be...as long as it aligns
with what God says about us too.

# September 13

*For God did not give us a spirit of timidity, but a spirit of power, of love and of self-discipline.*

2 TIMOTHY 1:7

# April 20

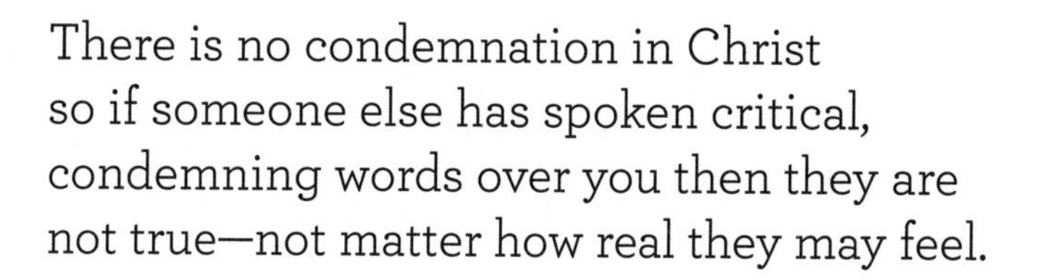

There is no condemnation in Christ
so if someone else has spoken critical,
condemning words over you then they are
not true—not matter how real they may feel.

# September 12

Fear can creep in at times even when we're doing exactly what God wants us to do in love. But if the only reason we're doing something is out of fear, then it's not from God.

# April 21

Until we're in heaven we won't see the complete picture—even about who we are. But we can begin to look into God's truth and ask him to show us what we need to know.

# September 11

*He who began a good work in you will carry it on to completion.*

PHILIPPIANS 1:6

# April 22

God has the ultimate word on who you are—not your spouse, friends, parents, coworkers, spiritual leaders, or even you. And he declares you're loved, valuable, accepted, and irreplaceable.
Did God really say...?

*Oh, yes, he did!*

# September 10

As you grow in love, you'll move more away from fear and toward love in different areas of your life.

# April 23

You question...
is who I am okay?
*You're more than okay—you're His.*
(Psalm 139:14)

# September 9

Being led by love is the cure
to being driven by fear.
“Perfect love drives out fear”
(1 John 4:18).

# April 24

You ask...
do I have what it takes?
*You've got all you need.*
(2 Peter 1:3)

# September 8

Hold on to the truth—you are loved,
accepted, enough in Christ.
Nothing and no one can take
that away from you.

# April 25

You wonder...
can I do this?
*You can do all things.*
(Philippians 4:13)

# September 7

You are not required to please people.
You don't have to meet their expectations.
You are a servant with *one* master.

# April 26

*Go for it, girl.*

Dare to make that difference,
take that step, follow that dream.
God will go with you—
and love will see you through.

# September 6

God is love—whatever he directs you to do will be loving to others too.

# April 27

*All* of our emotions are gifts from God to help us process *everything* we experience. Emotions are also a big part of what makes you amazing. They allow you to respond to life in deeply personal ways. They connect you with others. They reflect your awesome Maker.

# September 5

Ask God to continue uncovering the hidden expectations in your heart as well as the source. Also ask him to set you free from any that aren't truly from him.

# April 28

Research has shown that there are six universal emotions: anger, fear, disgust, amusement, sadness, and surprise. How we display those emotions shows up in facial expressions that are recognizable in even the most remote parts of the world.

# September 4

“After starting your Christian lives in the Spirit, why are you now trying to become perfect by your own human effort?” (Galatians 3:3) It’s a question we’re called to consider too. What expectations in our lives are from God—and what have we added as laws he never intended for us to be under?

# April 29

How we experience and express our feelings varies widely. Think of each basic emotion like a color. Give a box of crayons to a class of kindergartners and they'll all recognize red but use it in very different ways.

# September 3

*The Lord has told you what is good,*
*this is what he required of you:*
*to do what is right, to love mercy,*
*and to walk humbly with your God.*

MICAH 6:8

# April 30

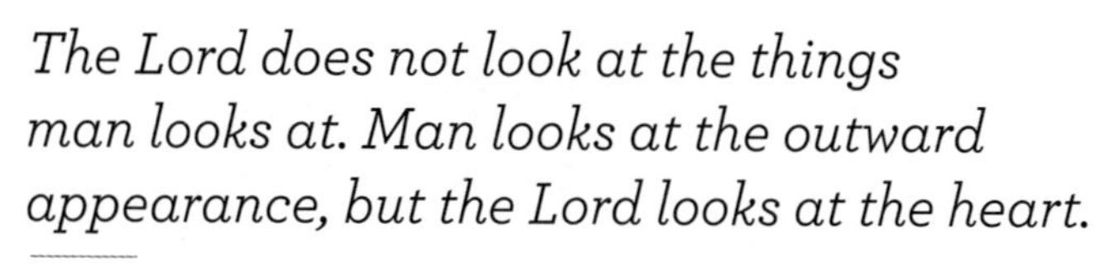

*The Lord does not look at the things man looks at. Man looks at the outward appearance, but the Lord looks at the heart.*

1 SAMUEL 16:7

# September 2

As servants, we're not in control of our own lives and we don't have to take orders from other servants either. Only God has the authority to tell us our duties, what's required of us.

# May 1

There's something about recognizing our quirks and differences that brings joy. I believe it does the same for God. After all, he's the one who created them.

# September 1

You're loved, accepted, set free
to live your life to the fullest.

# May 2

*O Lord, you have searched me and you know me. You know when I sit and when I rise; you perceive my thoughts from afar. You discern my going out and my lying down; you are familiar with all my ways. Before a word is on my tongue you know it completely, O Lord. You hem me in—behind and before; you have laid your hand upon me. Such knowledge is too wonderful for me, too lofty for me to attain.*

PSALM 139:1-6

# August 31

Your house doesn't have to be spotless.
Your work doesn't have to be flawless.
You don't have to please that
finicky member of your family.
You don't have to look like a
page out of a magazine.
You're already enough
because Jesus is enough in you.

Emotions make great messengers but bad bosses. If we listen to what the messenger has to share with us, turn to our Heavenly Father and ask, "What do you want me to do?" then all is well.

# August 30

We are not to be under anything but grace, the love of Christ, and the leading of the Holy Spirit.

# May 4

Our emotions speak into our lives.
They can share important information
with us about our experiences.
But God always gets the final say.

# August 29

*You are not under law, but under grace.*

ROMANS 6:14

# May 5

Emotion says, “Nobody cares.”
Truth says, “Jesus cares for me.”
Emotion says, “I’m angry and will show her!”
Truth says, “Be angry and sin not.”
Emotion says, “I’m afraid to hear
the doctor’s report.”
Truth says, “Fear not, for I am with you.”
Emotion says, “I can’t do this anymore.”
Truth says, “My grace is sufficient.”

PEGGY, *HEART TO HEART WITH HOLLEY* READER

## August 28

What's God's answer to expectations, to those laws we create for ourselves or let others lay down for us?

*Grace.*

# May 6

Every one of us thinks our normal is THE normal. Our way of life, responses, and yes, *emotions*, make sense to us. But ultimately, our reality has to be tested against God's ways of doing things. He says, "My thoughts are not your thoughts; neither are your ways my ways" (Isaiah 55:8).

# August 27

God can use you wherever you are
and in whatever you're doing.

God's intent is for us to appropriately experience the full range of emotions.

# August 26

It seems what God wants most
in our stories is our hearts.

# May 8

You are God's beautiful, loved, cherished daughter and he wants you to live fully.

# August 25

By understanding how we're created and called to express love, we find focus and direction. We can say "yes" to what matters most and "no" to what isn't necessary without guilt. We can make sure our days are spent wisely and we live well.

# May 9

When we look in the Bible, we see the full range of emotions—especially in the Psalms. David expresses everything from wild joy to deep sorrow. *And all of those honored God.* It's what we do with our emotions that matters. For example, "In your anger do not sin" (Ephesians 4:26).

# August 24

We're here to express faith through love—
for God, others, and ourselves.

# May 10

We all have a point at which we have to choose which evidence to believe. Do we rely on our emotions alone? Or do we look into God's truth and let him tell us what's real?

# August 23

As believers, we all ultimately have the same mission. God gave it to us in Galatians 5:6, “The only thing that counts is faith expressing itself through love.”

# May 11

At the end of the day, we've got to listen and follow God's Spirit more than our own hearts. He's the ultimate reality check.

# August 22

How is God asking you to live in love?
First with him and then with family, friends,
and others he's called you to serve.

# May 12

We need sisters of faith who will speak truth to us when we can't see it or simply don't have the strength to believe it in that moment. Seek out "Joshuas and Calebs" who will do more than just go shopping with you—they'll make sure you get to the Promised Land too.

# August 21

Love in a biblical sense isn't a touchy-feely, vague experience. It's a verb. It's a series of choices and actions in our lives.

*I can do everything through him who gives me strength.*

PHILIPPIANS 4:13

# August 20

God is love and *everything* he does is loving. "God is love. Whoever lives in love lives in God, and God in him" (1 John 4:16). What does God really want us to do with our lives? Not make them perfect. *Grow in love.*

# May 14

God promises to give us something to wear. And it's just right for our calling in life. We're not going to prom, ladies. We're going to a battlefield. That's why he tells us to guard our hearts and he's given us the armor of God to do so.

# August 19

In the New Testament, the Greek word for "perfect" is "teleios" and it's actually more accurately described as maturing growth or completion. For example, an oak tree is the "teleios" of an acorn, says Adrian Rogers.

# May 15

*Therefore put on the full armor of God, so that when the day of evil comes, you may be able to stand your ground, and after you have done everything, to stand. Stand firm then, with the belt of truth buckled around your waist, with the breastplate of righteousness in place, and with your feet fitted with the readiness that comes from the gospel of peace. In addition to all this, take up the shield of faith, with which you can extinguish all the flaming arrows of the evil one. Take the helmet of salvation and the sword of the Spirit, which is the word of God.*

EPHESIANS 6:13-17

# August 18

Psalm 18 stopped me in my tracks one day. It says, "God's way is perfect...and he makes my way perfect." Did you catch that? *You are not responsible for making yourself perfect.* God will do so—and his idea of perfect is entirely different than ours.

# May 16

The breastplate of righteousness covers the heart. And that's really what we've been talking about all along. "Above all else, guard your heart for it is the wellspring of life" (Proverbs 4:23). Emotions matter because our hearts affect *every other part of who we are and what we do.*

# August 17

I question, "God, don't you want
me to be busy all the time? Don't
you want me to push myself to
the limit for you and others?"
It seems my heart hears a whisper
in response, "Daughter, I did not
come to give you a full life. I came
to give you life to the full."

At first I didn't understand why righteousness would be what covers our hearts in the armor of God. But then it became clear—*when we choose to do what is right in spite of our emotions, it protects us.*

# August 16

Let's dare to love, to share life with each other, to offer ourselves in the way God has created us to do.

I need you.
You need me.
The Kingdom needs *us*.

# May 18

Think of times in your life when you've let your emotions get the best of you. I'm recalling some now and the first word that comes to mind is "ouch." Exactly. When we let our emotions get out of control we get hurt. And often others do too. When God says "Obey me rather than your emotions" he's really looking out for our best interests.

# August 15

*You are loved.*

You matter.
You have so much to give the world and the hearts in it.

# May 19

*Do not be anxious about anything, but in everything, by prayer and petition, with thanksgiving, present your requests to God. And the peace of God, which transcends all understanding, will guard your hearts and your minds in Christ Jesus.*

PHILIPPIANS 4:6-7

# August 14

*You, my brothers, were called to be free. But do not use your freedom to indulge the sinful nature; rather, serve one another in love.*

GALATIANS 5:13

# May 20

Worry is a sign that we're letting our emotions get the best of us. (And believe me, I know. When it comes to worrying, I'm a pro.) So when we start sensing those feelings taking over, God invites us to come to him instead.

# August 13

The part of ourselves that we're called to deny is the sin nature within us that wants its own way. We're never to use our strengths (or weaknesses) as an excuse for being selfish. Instead we're to see all of who we are as an invitation to serve.

When we say thanks along with our requests, we're reminding ourselves of what's true regardless of the circumstances at the moment (remember Joshua and Caleb?).

# August 12

Even when we live in our strengths, love still requires sacrifice. Jesus said that if we're going to follow him it means taking up our cross and denying ourselves. The point is that it's *our* cross—not someone else's. Jesus didn't say, "Take up your cross and deny who God made you."

# May 22

When we present our requests to God and give thanks, He says his peace, which is beyond all understanding, will guard our hearts. It's like a bullet proof vest that looks gorgeous too. Simply stunning.

# August 11

We're amazing not because of who we are but because of who lives within us.

# May 23

God made you an emotional being.
That's a beautiful, powerful, glorious thing.

# August 10

"Being led by the Holy Spirit" can sound vague or super-spiritual. But it's really just moment-by-moment, day-by-day dependence. It's acknowledging that even in our strengths, we need a lot of help. And even in our weaknesses, God can enable us to do more than we imagined.

## May 24

The reason we have emotions is because God has them too. We read in the Bible about him feeling everything from anger to sadness to joy.

# August 9

*Power* – We don't have to live in our strengths on our own. The Spirit is the one who enables us to do what we're called to do.
*Self-discipline* – In the times when we feel weak or inadequate, the Spirit will also give us what we need to do what God asks.
*Love* – Whatever God wants us to do is ultimately about love and the only way we can love like he does is through the Spirit within us.

# May 25

We have the capacity to reflect God through our emotions because we're created in his image—every part of us. Those tears you cry. That smile you give. The anger you express at injustice.

# August 8

The Spirit enables us to live the way God wants and to be all he's created us to be. "For God did not give us a spirit of timidity, but a spirit of power, of love and of self-discipline" (2 Timothy 1:7).

God has given you a wardrobe of emotions fit for a princess because that's what you are in his eyes. Wear them royally, with your heart held high, and show the world what it means to be a passionate woman who has the courage to truly experience life and express herself (and the One who knows her heart best) with love and grace through it all.

# August 7

Jesus invites us to a better way. He says we don't have to go through life in our own power anymore. Instead he promises that when we belong to him the Holy Spirit comes to live within us. The Spirit is many things to us—a guide, comforter, counselor, and the one who leads us into all truth. He's the every day, every moment companion of our hearts.

# May 27

I'm imagining a car pulling up to the curb.
You step out of it, confidently
placing your feet on the red
carpet of God's plans for you.
I wave wildly, snap a picture,
and smile from deep inside.
*Oh, girl, your heart is looking*
*fabulous today.*

# August 6

Here's the thing—God's not the only one with a plan for your life. The enemy has one too. And if he can't get you to rebel outright, then sidetracking you and getting you outside of your strengths is a pretty good alternative. You are of incredible worth to the Kingdom. Dare to be who you are, who God created you to be.

# May 28

Before we know where we're going we need to understand where we are at the moment.

# August 5

No one can take your place.
God doesn't have a "plan B" for you.
You have gifts to offer the world, ways of connecting, that only you can fulfill.

# May 29

*Whenever the cloud lifted from above the Tent, the Israelites set out; wherever the cloud settled, the Israelites encamped. At the Lord's command the Israelites set out, and at his command they encamped.*

NUMBERS 9:17-18

# August 4

*Now the body is not made up of one part but of many. If the foot should say, "Because I am not a hand, I do not belong to the body," it would not for that reason cease to be part of the body. And if the ear should say, "Because I am not an eye, I do not belong to the body," it would not for that reason cease to be part of the body. If the whole body were an eye, where would the sense of hearing be? If the whole body were an ear, where would the sense of smell be? But in fact God has arranged the parts in the body, every one of them, just as he wanted them to be.*

1 CORINTHIANS 12:14-18

# May 30

The cloud above the temple was God's presence. So to sum all that up, *wherever God went the Israelites went too*. He asks us to do the same in our lives. Our role isn't to rush ahead but instead to stay right by his side.

# August 3

We often try to force ourselves to be like others or to simply do whatever we're asked. Then we wonder why we feel ineffective and exhausted. We are the body of Christ—and that means we not only have individual strengths to offer; we also have unique ways of loving others.

# May 31

We feel like we need to do more, less, or something entirely different than everyone else. We end up zigzagging from spot to spot on the map and wear ourselves out in the process. All the while God is saying, "Dear daughter, I'm here, right here. Won't you join me?"

# August 2

When we think about the biblical command to “love one another” it seems like the way we go about doing so should be one-size-fits-all. But the way God expresses his love through you will look entirely different than the way he does it through someone else.

# June 1

Here's the good news: God has a journey for YOUR life. It looks different than anyone else's. The road he's carved out for you is yours alone. It's always the road less traveled because you're the only one who is ever going to walk it.

# August 1

We sigh and ask, “Why do I act this way?” The beautiful answer to that question just may be, “Because that’s exactly how God made you, sweet girl.”

# June 2

Oh, sure, God will give you wonderful traveling companions to go with you. But don't let that fool you—that doesn't mean their paths are the same as yours—just that they're parallel for a time.

# July 31

Control keeps us alone. God invites us instead to love—to that wild, unknown, heart-pounding reality of relationships. We're to give him the reigns of our hearts and then he loves others through us.

# June 3

Your GPS (God Positioning System) is going to get *you* exactly where you need to go. And he promises to be with you every step of the way.

# July 30

To love at all is to be vulnerable. Love anything, and your heart will certainly be wrung and possibly broken. If you want to make sure of keeping it intact, you must give your heart to no one, not even to an animal. Wrap it carefully round with hobbies and little luxuries; avoid all entanglements; lock it up safe in the casket or coffin of your selfishness. But in that casket—safe, dark, motionless, airless—it will change. It will not be broken; it will become unbreakable, impenetrable, irredeemable.

C.S. LEWIS

# June 4

*The Lord delights in those who fear him,*
*who put their hope in his unfailing love.*

PSALM 147:11

# July 29

God will help us guard our hearts.
"He is my loving God and my fortress,
my stronghold and my deliverer, my shield,
in whom I take refuge" (Psalm 144:2).
God wants to be your protection.

# June 5

We all begin our journeys in the same spot the Israelites did—Egypt. Most biblical scholars believe that Egypt, a place of slavery, represents how we're all born into sin. We're controlled by it. Then God comes along and promises to set us free.

# July 28

As a child playing hide and seek, I remember one person would eventually yell, "Olly olly oxen free!" I still have no idea what that means but it seems God makes the same declaration to our hearts: it's safe to come out of hiding. In the game of life, we're free, loved, found forever.

# June 6

If you haven't started a relationship with God yet then you can do so right now by giving your life to him. Just tell him something like:

God, I believe you exist, that you love me, and that you sent your son to die on the cross for my sins. I ask your forgiveness for those sins and I receive your gift of a right relationship with you and eternal life forever in heaven. All I am and all I have is now yours. Amen.

# July 27

*No more Hide and Seek.* God seems to prefer *Seek and Find.* "You will seek me and find me when you seek me with all your heart" (Jeremiah 29:13). Here's how it works: We come out of hiding and then we're free to pursue God's heart, chase his will, freely follow his path for our lives.

# June 7

If you've given your life to God, you're his always. Sometimes we just need to stop and realign with his direction for our lives again. You can start that by praying something like this:
Lord, thank you that I am yours and that you have a plan for my life. I've gotten off track. Please forgive me. I want to make a u-turn right now. I want to be where you are and live in Your presence. Help me change. Amen.

## July 26

Insecurity makes me hide emotionally.
God asks my heart, "Why are you hiding?"
On any given day, the answer varies.
But his response is always the same—
to call me back to confidence in him,
remind me of who I am, bring me
back into the light of his love.

# June 8

God's grace is your highway out of Egypt and on to better things. As Karen, a reader on my blog *Heart to Heart with Holley*, powerfully declared, "The same God who delivered me from the sins of my past will deliver me from the sins of my present!"

# July 25

If you've felt afraid to put yourself out there because you feel less than perfect, because you're afraid what others might say, then reach out your hands and open your heart, sweet sister. You are already perfectly loved and you only have to please the One who has already declared you are a delight to his heart.

I'm a "let's get on the road" kind of girl. Yes, ma'am. Pack up those tents, put them in the car, and let's go! There have been multiple times in my life when God's direction to me has clearly been the worst four-letter word of all in my vocabulary—*wait*.

As I look back over those times, I can see that waiting was indeed part of the overall plan and served a purpose.

# July 24

We're called to care about others, to be kind and considerate, to try our best to bless them. But, ladies, we don't have to make everyone happy. *And if we don't have to make everyone happy then we don't have to be perfect.* God has already declared us good enough, worthy in his sight, valuable and with much to offer the world.

# June 10

Making progress in life is hard work. When we insist on moving forward as quickly as possible, we can wear ourselves out in a hurry. Sometimes when God makes us wait it's one of the most merciful things he can do.

# July 23

*Am I now trying to win the approval of men, or of God? Or am I trying to please men? If I were still trying to please men, I would not be a servant of Christ.*

GALATIANS 1:10

# June 11

Waiting doesn't inherently mean we've done something wrong. In fact, it can indicate just the opposite—that we're right between some really big things God has for our lives and we need to rest up.

# July 22

I protested, "But God, I want people to like me. I want people to be happy with me. Isn't that what it means to be loving?" And as I dug deeper into his Word it became clear that, no, being loving doesn't mean pleasing people. *We are to love people but we're only asked to please God.*

# June 12

God knows we're human. He knows we get worn out. Sometimes he simply says, "Take a break, child."

## July 21

I'm slowly learning it's not about being perfect...but being perfectly loved. There is no fear in love. But perfect love drives out fear (1 John 4:18).

# June 13

I have friends with young kids and naptime doesn't ever seem to be very welcome. There's usually some protesting. But in the end, my friends make sure their little ones get the rest they need for their own good. We can be like those reluctant kids too. We're so set on getting where we want to go that the last thing we want to do is nap (or encamp). But our Heavenly Father in his infinite tenderness knows that sometimes that's exactly what we need most.

## July 20

*Love all. Please One.*
*Be who I've created you to be.*
*You are enough because*
*I am enough in you.*

# June 14

Life's hard. We get hurt. That means sometimes what we need most is for God to stop us right in the middle of our road as we limp along and say, "Daughter, sit down. Rest. Heal. Let me tend to your wounds."

# July 19

The world needs you as a woman
to do what only you can do,
to love the way only you can love,
to offer what you have to share.
Believe me, sister, it's beautiful and worth
much—more than you can even imagine.

# June 15

Jesus seems to whisper to my heart, "*If I will wash your feet, will I not wash your wounds*?" I have a choice. Drop my guard or guard my hurts.

We, as women,
often do go to battle.

We fight cancer.
We fight for our marriages.
We fight for our children.
And in doing so, *we help*.

# June 16

We want to move forward in our lives.
We want to keep saying "I'm fine" and
pressing ahead as if that's really true.
But Jesus in his infinite love for us
sometimes slows us down for a season
so that he can heal our hearts.

# July 17

The word for “helper” is the same word often used when God helps us. David uses it in the Psalms, “We wait in hope for the Lord; he is our help and our shield” (Psalm 33:20). Here the help that comes from God is the kind one needs in war—it stands side-by-side with a shield.

# June 17

God's plans for our lives take preparation.
That's not my favorite part—I just
want to get to the end result.
But sometimes God asks us to "encamp"
so that he can do the necessary work
in our lives for his purposes.

# July 16

Think of the women in your life. Encouraging, comforting, cooking, painting, working...it's almost all for someone else. They labor on behalf of love. This "helping" varies in its intensity. Sometimes it's a soft hand brushed across the hot brow of a sick child. But often it's fierce, strong, wild, bold.

Ladies, I know none of us like this but it's just got to be said—sometimes *it's just not time yet*. There's no logical explanation for the delay. God is simply doing his thing. "For my thoughts are not your thoughts, neither are your ways My ways, declares the Lord" (Isaiah 55:8).

# July 15

When we think of Eve being created as a "helper" for Adam, we tend to assume that word describes her role. But what if it's much deeper than that? What if it describes her heart?

# June 19

God offers this hope: "He who began a good work in you will carry it on to completion until the day of Christ Jesus" (Philippians 1:6). In other words, whatever journey God begins in your life and heart, he promises to finish—in his perfect timing.

# July 14

As the daughters of Eve, being made to share life with others is especially true of us—it's central to what makes each of us amazing. God created Eve with relationships in mind.

# June 20

Ecclesiastes 3:11 says, God "has made everything beautiful in its time. He has also set eternity in the hearts of men; yet they cannot fathom what God has done from beginning to end." That verse speaks to what it's like to be in the mysterious middle—of circumstances, unmet expectations, the journey from Egypt to Home. When we're in the "middle" of life we can take comfort in knowing we're right in the center of God's hands too.

Why was Adam being alone not good? *Because it's not like God.*

Father.
Son.
Holy Spirit.

The Kingdom we serve is one of love, relationship, and intimacy. We're not made *for* each other but we're certainly made to share life *with* each other.

# June 21

You are loved. God has a purpose for you.
He is working out his plans for your life.
And just when you least expect it, you'll
be on your way so he can take you
all the way to the Promised Land.

# July 12

Wanting other people in your life isn't weakness. Instead it's a reflection that you are created by a God who is inherently relational. Look at the lengths he's gone to just to have a relationship with you.

# June 22

*The Lord replied, "My Presence will go with you, and I will give you rest."*

EXODUS 33:14

# July 11

When God says being alone "isn't good" the contrast is stark. Remember the seven days of creation? After sky, water, birds, animals, light, dark, God says, "It is good." And yet now he is announcing the opposite. A life without relationships with other human beings isn't good—isn't what he planned.

# June 23

It seemed God gently whispered to my heart, "*If you're driven, you can't be led.*"

We may tell ourselves, “If only I were closer to God I wouldn’t feel like I needed other people so much.” But Adam lived in a perfect place. There was no sin. He had an intimacy with God we can only imagine. Yet God still said that Adam being alone wasn’t good.

# June 24

We can be driven by all kinds of things—fear, insecurities, ambition, pride, comparison, or lies from our childhood. But we can only be led by one Person.

# July 9

It seems God created within us a deep desire to share life with each other—flesh and blood. In the Garden of Eden he declared, “It’s not good for man to be alone.” It’s not good for woman either. We need others to speak truth to us, remind us we’re amazing, walk alongside us and encourage us in all God has called us to do.

# June 25

Jesus promised the Holy Spirit would "lead us into all truth" (John 16:13). Instead of God's presence being a cloud above the temple like it was for the Israelites on the way to the Promised Land, we have God's presence within us. "Your body is a temple of the Holy Spirit" (1 Corinthians 6:19).

You won't be where you are forever. God promises when you trust him that he'll take care of you wherever you are and get you where he wants you to go.

# June 26

Make a habit of asking God to speak to you and then listening for his voice in your life. As you do, make sure what you hear lines up with God's Word—anything that's from him always will.

# July 7

*The Lord your God is bringing you into a good land—a land with streams and pools of water, with springs flowing in the valleys and hills; a land with wheat and barley, vines and fig trees, pomegranates, olive oil and honey; a land where bread will not be scarce and you will lack nothing....When you have eaten and are satisfied, praise the Lord your God for the good land he has given you.*

DEUTERONOMY 8:7-10

# June 27

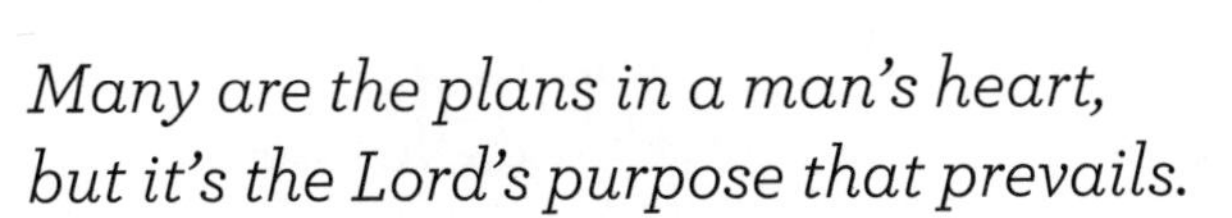

*Many are the plans in a man's heart,*
*but it's the Lord's purpose that prevails.*

PROVERBS 19:26

# July 6

Once we're in our Promised Land, God wants us to enjoy it! After wandering in the wilderness so long, our joy muscles can get a little weak. Give yourself permission to celebrate where God has brought you and what he has entrusted to you.

# June 28

"But those who wait on the Lord shall renew their strength; they shall mount up with wings like eagles, they shall run and not be weary, they shall walk and not faint." It's clear from those words that this kind of waiting isn't passive—it's more about *keeping pace with God.*

# July 5

When we get to where God is taking us, it doesn't mean we can get so comfortable that we let our guards down or neglect our relationship with him. Gratitude and obedience are the best defenses for our Promised Land.

# June 29

When God asks us to set out, we can get so focused on moving forward, on getting to the Promised Land, that we forget that the real point of the journey is our relationship. Yes, God moves us forward but most of all he simply wants *us*.

# July 4

Like Joshua and Caleb, we're to believe that the Promised Land will ultimately belong to us but the way that actually happens usually takes time and courage on our part.

# June 30

It can seem hard to believe at times but it's true—the God of the Universe wants to share life with you. Every step. Every day. All the way to your forever home with him.

# July 3

When the Israelites arrive at the edge of the Promised Land, God tells them to go in and make it fully theirs. He asks us to do the same too. That can take a lot of hard work and fighting some battles. Possessing the Promised Land isn't a one-time event but instead a process.

# July 1

*Have I not commanded you? Be strong and courageous. Do not be terrified; do not be discouraged, for the Lord your God will be with you wherever you go.*

JOSHUA 1:9

# July 2

For believers, heaven is the ultimate Promised Land. But God gave the Israelites a Promised Land in this life as well. I believe he often does the same for us too. Let's define a Promised Land as this: *A desire of your heart that God guides you into through an intimate journey with him.*